# A WORDSWORTH HANDBOOK

# *CASTLES*

*Wordsworth Editions*

First published in England 1994 by
Wordsworth Editions Ltd
Cumberland House
Crib Street
Ware
Hertfordshire SG12 9ET

ISBN 1–85326–815–1

*Right: **Arundel Castle***

*Previous page: **Henry VIII's artillery fort at St Mawes***

Designed and produced by Superlaunch Ltd
P O Box 207, Abingdon, Oxfordshire OX13 6TA, England
Text conversion and pagination by
August Filmsetting, St Helens, England
Colour separation by Seagull Reproductions Ltd, London
Printed and bound in the Czech Republic by Svoboda

# CONTENTS

## WHY BUILD A CASTLE?

All castles and forts, no matter when built, were intended as bases of active operation. The image of the castle as a stronghold, protected by an army, portcullis, drawbridge, moat and walls, its needs fulfilled by weapon makers and cooks from huge stores deep in the castle's inner sanctum, is not too far from the truth.

The component parts of a castle must include quarters for the master of the stronghold, providing somewhere for him to live and from which to conduct his schemes, and to store what is most valuable to him. Also essential are the judgement chamber for the trial of transgressors, quarters for the bodyguard to live and train in, and areas for storing their armament and also provisions. Externally, the castle must impress, portraying an impregnable mass. It needs the all-important tall observation towers, a complicated entrance arrangement and ample well-sited firing positions for archers. Outside, the castle's cavalry could patrol for a radius of 15km (9.32 miles) and infantry patrols up to 6km (3.73 miles). Longbowmen were effective up to 200m (356ft 2.4in), and a crossbow bolt could pierce armour at 350m (1,148ft 4.2in).

## HOW EARLY CASTLES WERE BUILT

Even since the earliest times, we have felt the need to protect what is ours, whether that was from marauding rivals or from wild beasts. Early peoples, probably semi-nomadic, with herds or farmland to protect, dug a perimeter ditch, piling the soil inside the excavated boundary. Reinforcements in the form of sticks or stones were added to the spoil heap, or a thorn hedge planted at the top. If they then moved on to fresher pastures or soil, returning a few years later, this same structure would still exist and need little refurbishment. Dead thorn bushes could be thrown into the trench, making it still more impassable, and a new hedge planted. Such a system is still practised by African tribes like the Masai.

The first hill-forts were the creation of the Neolithic peoples, who built causewayed camps. These were formed by a series of concentric ditches each up to 2m (6ft 6.7in) deep, bridged by numerous causeways giving easy access from every direction to the central circular enclosure, surrounded

## *Longbowmen outside Lincoln Castle*

by a bank topped by a palisade.

As the Bronze Age gave way to the Iron Age, new possibilities opened up to any local chief able to secure the services of a smith. The attraction of not only being able to make their own money but also durable and effective weapons turned both the British Isles and Europe into a vast perpetual battlefield, covered with a patchwork of little kingdoms in which the simple ringwork castles were built. These primarily comprised the domestic buildings of the chief's resi-

dence, and were encircled by a ditch. The soil from this, when piled round its inner edge, formed a rampart onto which a further breastwork was built, adding another 2m (6ft 6.7in) to the defences.

These works were often sited on a favoured existing isolated hilltop or on the projecting spur of a ridge, and as more experience was gained so the fortifications improved. The rampart created when digging the ditch was built further back from the edge, to leave a level space between them. The pile of rubble from the ditch formed by heaving the larger rocks and boulders into place was then

covered over by the accumu-
lated rubble, creating a flat top
to the rampart and a bank sloping down to the centre of the
enclosure. The outer edge of the
rampart eventually was made
vertical and surmounted by a
palisade and that was then
backed by a walkway.

At Murcens in Lot-et-
Garonne, south-west France,
and at Cadbury Castle near
Yeovil, Somerset, England, the
wooden stockage at the top of
the rampart was built as an
integral part of the earth bank.
Post-holes were dug, big
enough to take vertical timbers of 150mm (5.9in) which
were joined by rows of horizon-
tal timbers at 1.2m (3ft 11in)
intervals. These were supported by cross-timbers to rear
supports, thereby forming an **h**
in cross-section. The structure
was then filled in with earth and
rubble, the spoil of the ditch,
and faced at the front with a
layer of stones.

It was important to keep the
hilltop fortification in good
repair, and this included the
clearing out of the ditch and
keeping the sides straight. The
ditch tended to become littered
with soil and *débris*, which
when removed could be thrown
onto the outer perimeter,
where it formed another obstacle. Later on, a second such

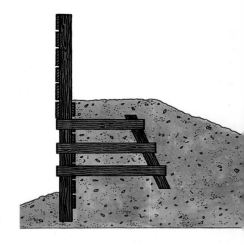

*Cross-sections showing how the*
*ramparts at Cadbury Castle were*
*constructed,* **top** *a wooden wall*
*with earth infill and* **below** *a*
*wooden palisade and rampart*
*wall*

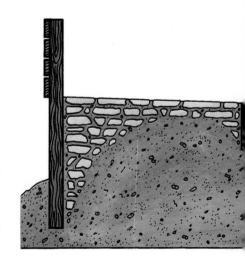

perimeter ditch was built, and sometimes a third, making the distance for the attackers from safe cover to the fortified walls more hazardous, and their attempt to enter even more susceptible to failure.

## GATEHOUSES AND OTHER OBSTACLES

The entrance through these defences was protected by a wooden gatehouse, possibly as much as 5m (16ft 5in) square, and 8m (26ft 3in) high, although the very large ringworks had even larger gatehouses. They also often had false gates, to confuse the attacker. The real gatehouse enclosed narrow obstructed alleyways which twisted and divided, some leading to blank walls, or into ditches. Beyond the outer gate and corridor was the inner door, often fronted by a deep ditch spanned by a simple moveable or destructible wooden bridge. Most of the hill-forts were large enough to contain herds of cattle, and all had ample storage pits to provide the fort's inhabitants with provisions against a lengthy seige. In addition, these hill forts were also self-contained units which had their own industries, the potters and smiths being the most important. The best of these,

being such a valuable asset, were probably confined to the fort.

## THE ROMANS ARE COMING

This ringwork method was the basis for 400 years of military campaigns by the Roman Empire. After a day's march, or less if a suitable campsite was found, the survey party staked out the centre line of the camp some 30m (98ft 5in) across, with a cross-line forming a second pathway, and marked the positions for the tents. When the soldiers arrived, they immediately shed most of their equipment and began work digging a ditch. Normally this was 3.5m (11ft 5.8in) wide and 2.5m (8ft 2.4in) deep. The excavated soil was thrown onto the inner rim to form a rampart covered on its outer wall with thorn bushes, with a palisade of sharpened stakes rammed into the top. Meanwhile, the mule train arrived and the tents were unrolled and pitched. Each skin tent housed eight soldiers.

Guards were posted and their shifts rotated at three-hourly intervals. The following morning, or possibly the next, the legion would move on, deserting the fortification. If a longer stay should ever be necessary, these fortifications could be

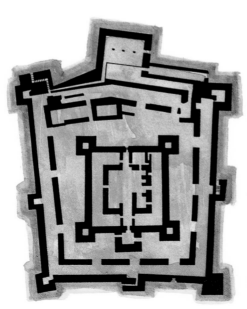

*Belvoir Castle was dependent upon the Roman model for its design, with square towers at the angles in the Roman manner and a great gate tower centrally placed on the western wall. An outer enclosure was added, with interval towers along the curtain wall, connected behind a wide fighting platform. There is no central keep; the original plan left is shown here at right angles to the photograph above*

8

strengthened with stone walls and elevated observation stations provided. The soldiers could then leave to conduct patrols or to engage in battle, correctly clad and with the knowledge that if necessary they could always retreat to their stronghold and regroup.

When conquered territories were peacefully occupied, these temporary summer camps could be easily converted to more permanent structures with purpose-built wooden barrack blocks replacing the tents.

## THE SCIENCE OF WAR

When the Romans invaded Britain in 43AD, the hill-forts were systematically destroyed by Roman seigecraft, the likes of which had never been experienced in Britain before. Devices used included *scorpiones*, large crossbows firing metal bolts; *ballistae*, catapults hurling rocks and timber with a higher trajectory, capable of smashing timber palisades and huts; *grapnels* attached to the front of swinging beams used from seige towers to rip away masonry and palisades; and *testudines*, large shield-like structures which protected the seige engineers' backs.

There are stories of outstand-

ing resistance to Roman seiges. At Avaricum, a hill-fort city in what is now Bourges, France, such defiance was shown that when the city eventually fell, only 800 of the 40,000 inhabitants were spared the sword. Similarly Vespasian bombarded into defeat Maċ Dun or Maiden Castle, in Dorset, England. At Masada, a hill-top refuge overlooking the Dead Sea and surrounded by a curtain wall, a three-year seige was finally ended by the defenders killing their wives, their children and then themselves, after laying out their store of food to show that they had not been starved out, and were prepared to succumb neither to the sword nor to domination.

## WILLIAM THE CONQUEROR

When the Normans came to England in 1066 and Duke William landed at Pevensey, the first thing he did was to build a temporary castle for himself in what remained of an original Roman fort. At Hastings he built a second, and at Dover a third, a refortification of an earthworks. Within a year, London was secured by castles and as the Norman campaign swept through England, he built at Exeter in the west, at York and Durham in the north,

at Warwick, Lincoln, Huntingdon and Nottingham in the midlands, and at many more cities, with the express purpose of overawing the populace. These castles became the forward base in the subjugation of the countryside. Later, these same castles became homes, treasuries, or even administrative centres and prisons.

The first Norman castles built in England were like those of the Roman legions, temporary overnight encampments of a ditch with a wooden wall erected on the earth excavated from the ditch. To save time and labour, they took with them a prefabricated castle, and indeed had originally transported such a castle to England in 1066. These prefabricated castles could be easily dismantled in the morning, stowed in a wagon and ready for the column of soldiers to set off again.

**Left: *the White Tower of HM Tower of London, built by William the Conqueror; Henry I's Bishop of Durham was its first prisoner. It served as an armoury, a garrison, and a royal palace, abolished by Cromwell. Other inmates included kings of Scotland, France and England, Lady Jane Grey, Sir Thomas More and Elizabeth I***

## MOTTE AND BAILEY

The motte and bailey castles developed next. The motte, a conical mound, was built either with rocks and earth quarried from the encircling ditch, or by shaping the sides of a conveniently-sited knoll. These mounds, and the buildings placed on them, varied greatly in size, but they would have carried at least a small tower with limited accommodation.

The bailey, at ground level beside the motte and encircled by the same dry ditch, was also defended by a rampart which was sometimes encased in timber. Ideally kidney-shaped in plan, allowing its area to be covered by bow-shot from the motte, the bailey enclosed most of the castle's domestic buildings. Usually these comprised a hall for formal use, a kitchen, forge, and armoury, together with stables and barns.

Access between the motte and bailey was purposely difficult, and the Bayeux Tapestry depicts 'flying' bridges being used to reach the top of the motte. At other castles, tunnels were dug deep into the basement of the towers or steep steps cut into the side of the motte.

These motte and bailey

*Tamworth Castle above is a typical Norman motte and bailey castle. Its sandstone walls and superb herringbone wall are thought to date from the 1180s. They replaced a palisade and wooden tower on the present artificial mound (motte) with an enclosure (lower bailey), which would have been constructed shortly after the Norman Conquest*

designs were the more permanent fortifications built by the Normans, using local peasant labour. Their name shows Norman origins, 'motte' being from the French word for turf. The mound upon which the house was built often contained the cellar or dungeon, an anglicised corruption of the word donjon. The ditch surrounding the mound was later referred to as the motte, and again was anglicised, being transcribed as moat.

## KEEPS

Shell keeps were the next to appear, at the end of the 11th century. Built to replace wooden palisades on mottes, these stone structures basically encased the existing motte in stone, usually uncoursed and often undressed. The entrance to a shell keep was usually just a simple doorway in the wall, although in some instances a small tower might command the entrance. Rooms were arranged around the inside of the walls, with a central, usually circular, courtyard.

The success of these stone-built fortresses led to the simple square keep. This was no more than a stone hall, raised to first-floor level and entered at that level via a flight of steps.

At ground level, the thick walls featured slit windows. Enlarged by placing a second chamber adjacent to and paral-

lel with the hall, these hall keeps were also plain on the outside but showed development, being two storeys high with pilaster buttresses added. Spiral stairs in each corner led from the first-floor entrance up to the battlements and down to the ground-floor basement.

The tower keep evolved at much the same time. These had a much smaller base area, often as little as $20m^2$ (39.2sq yds), but they rose to three or four storeys in height. The outer walls, much like those of the hall keeps, tended to be decorated by pilaster strips rising from a splayed plinth, which not only had the effect of spreading the load of the walls, but also provided additional protection at ground level against attack by battering rams. The corners of these keeps were usually strengthened by using closely-placed

*The tower keep of Provins as it is now, shown in plan and section*

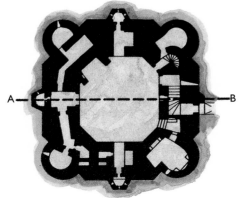

pilasters, buttresses or even corner turrets, which then rose above the main roof level. The roofs were almost flat, and because of the span involved, two parallel roofs were required. The outer walls rose above the roof, serving both as a parapet and as protection from fire arrows. Battlements were also a common feature, as were hourds. Windows were tall and narrow, especially at ground level, and many were arrow-loops.

Entry to tower keeps, in common with virtually all keeps, was generally at first-floor level, approached by stairs built against the outer wall. The entrance to the forebuilding, projecting from the side of the keep and enclosing the stairs, was protected by a door and portcullis with additional protection often being given by the inclusion of a pit halfway up the stairs, crossed by a draw-bridge. Occasionally entry to the keep was at second-floor level, so as to provide extra space for the inclusion of the added defences.

Entering the keep via the stairs and forebuilding, you might arrive in the hall, which in other tower keeps might have been entered through a small lobby. In larger tower keeps, this floor would be divided by a crosswall and would contain the stairs to the basement and second floor, latrines and a chapel. The second floor would contain another large hall, private bedchambers and latrines, possibly a second chapel and kitchens, though these would not be elaborate. Heating was by open fires, with the flues rising through the thickness of the walls to the roof. The windows on this upper floor were larger than those below.

A century after the Norman conquest of England, castles had developed as far as the round and polygonal keeps, built from a circular ground plan with large rectangular turrets projecting from the walls to produce a more interesting and complicated layout. Although entrance was still at first-floor level, there was generally no forebuilding. The internal stairs were a single spiral running from the ground floor to the roof, but apart from these apparent differences and the often more elaborate layout of the space the arrangements floor-by-floor were similar to those of the square keeps.

### Hedingham Castle

The Castle's great Norman keep, illustrated *right*, is

among the most magnificent and best presented in Europe, built by Aubrey de Vere in about 1140.

The immensely strong walls of the keep are 3.66m (12ft) at the base, narrowing to 3.05m (10ft) at the top. The east wall is 304.8mm (1ft) thicker than the other three, probably to give additional protection against attacks from the bridge side. The facing stone is ashlar, transported all the way from quarries in Northamptonshire, and Hedingham is one of the very few Norman castles in England to be completely faced with stone, this being partly because of the prohibitive cost caused by the transportation problems. Within the inner and outer facing is an infill of local flints and rubble bound together with a mortar, made of sand, lime and water.

The small holes that appear on the exterior were for fixing the wooden scaffolding poles during the original building while the regularly-spaced gaps near the battlements are put-log holes. These housed the beams thrust through the wall to support wooden planks and hoardings, which provided the archers with far greater mobility and a wider field of fire. Also the planks could be removed, which would enable molten

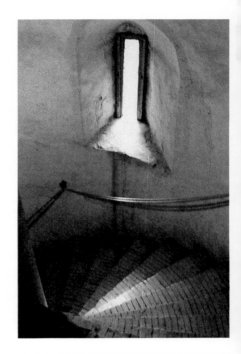

*A view down the spiral stair at Hedingham*

pitch or boiling oil to be poured down upon the enemy.

The original castle was built with an inner and outer bailey, with the keep and other important buildings being in the inner bailey. Both had a curtain wall built round them. Today on the eastern approach a Tudor bridge, built in 1496, spans the dry moat, replacing the drawbridge which joined the inner and outer baileys.

The Castle surroundings were kept clear of all scrub and trees so that the approaching enemy were conceded no cover. The trees which exist today were planted in the early 18th century, when Hedingham finally became a gentleman's residence, rather than a military fortification. Other alterations made at the same time included the two entrances that were knocked into the east side of the keep. From the bridge (originally the drawbridge), a path crosses the inner bailey to the west side of the keep, and a stone staircase leads up to a splendid arched doorway. The stone steps were originally covered by a protection to the main entrance from such

**Left: *a typical Norman archway***

weapons as battering rams, and in effect made direct attack impossible.

The roofless chamber outside the front door is the dungeon, a dark and gloomy hole into which the unlucky prisoners were lowered through a trap door in the ceiling.

The main doorway has a well defined typical Norman chevron moulding above it, which is repeated on the exterior above the top windows and in the banqueting hall. A portcullis used to slide down from over the door, operated by a system of winches from the floor above. Today, the grooves in which the portcullis slid are still visible, as are the holes cut into the walls at the side of the doorway into which draw bars were slid to give reinforcement. The entrance to the keep is on the first floor; again this was a device to make attack harder. It opened into the garrison or guardroom where the soldiers lived. On the same level were the armourer's forge and the kitchens. Windows at first-floor level are very narrow, allowing archers to fire through, but allowing in only a very little light.

The garderobe or lavatory is situated in the north-east corner, and from the north-west corner a spiral staircase leads down to the ground floor and up to the banqueting hall. The staircase is 3.965m (13ft) wide in circumference and beautifully constructed around a central column. The original stone steps were replaced with bricks in the 16th century. The staircase was built in a clockwise direction to allow the defending soldiers a free right hand with which to wield their swords as they descended.

There are no windows on the ground floor, which was used for the storage of food and provisions. The walls here are very thick, and keep the temperature within cool and constant; the keep also had its own well.

The second floor comprises the banqueting hall or armoury. It has a splendid timbered ceiling, supported by a magnificent central arch 8.54m (28ft) wide and rising to a height of 6.1m (20ft).

On the south wall is sited the fireplace, designed with a cone-shaped flue which contains two ducts near the top. These run straight through the wall and emerge on either side of a flat buttress. This meant that if the wind caused the fire to smoke, one or other of the openings could be blocked, depending on the direction of the wind. As with the first floor, the northeast corner houses the upper

extension of the garderobe shaft. Access to the portcullis winding mechanism was gained to the right of the stairs, near the entrance to the room. The great hall was used for entertaining, granting of audiences and holding court. At 3.66m (12ft) above floor level a gallery runs around the entire room, tunnelled within the thickness of the walls, from which the minstrels and the troubadors would have played.

The room would have been simply furnished with trestle tables, benches and chests placed on a floor covered in rushes. The walls were hung with richly-decorated woven hangings.

Above this was the dormitory floor, a large room divided by rugs and hangings. Whereas the lord and his lady would have had simple wooden beds, most other people slept on straw on the floor, while the soldiers and servants slept on the floors below, wherever they could find space.

## BUILT IN STONE

The transition to stone as the choice for castle building was very rapid. The techniques were used across the entire gamut of buildings, from ecclesiastical – such as cathedrals, monasteries and even parish churches – down to demotic architecture, long before the end of the 12th century.

A stone-built castle was now a necessity, the developing science of seigecraft had seen to that, and by the end of the 12th century this quite radical change in the principles of castle building was evident.

Initially stone towers and keeps followed the style employed when building in timber, with the consequence that the sheer weight of some towers led them to collapse. However, the rectangular keep was to become a feature of the early 12th-century castle, now rapidly evolving into a sophisticated building; so much so, that legislation was often used to limit their building.

One of the most advanced early buildings of the period was the tower keep at Houdan (Ile-de-France), cylindrical in plan and with four angle turrets. It dates from about 1125. Its one drawback was in the provision of flanking fire, as the continuing curve of the keep's main wall hid large areas of its base from view.

Another interesting development was the creation by William d'Aubigny, the Earl of Arundel, at Castle Rising in Norfolk, England, of an ornate square keep. This was the largest in England by the middle of the 12th century. It is a hall keep of two floors, the upper floor being residential, providing hall, kitchen, chapel and gallery. The keep was built in the centre of a ringwork, thereby duplicating the defensive strengths of an existing keep by building the new one inside it.

The most economical method was to rebuild in stone over the existing timber structure, gradually reinforcing it while retaining its outer fortifications.

This happened not only in England. Gisors, in Normandy, France, is an interesting example of an 11th-century motte later crowned by a very large shell keep. A great tower was subsequently added by Henry II, after which Gisors fell to the French, and Philip Augustus built another tower away from the motte but commanding the main gate. The tower keeps of the Capetian line of kings, of which Gisors is one, must take their place in revealing Philip Augustus as being among the great castle builders.

These tower keeps were becoming more experimental in design by the late 12th century, and the groundswell of transition was apparent.

The traditional square and

*The tower keep of Villeneuve-sur-Yonne, built by Philip Augustus, provided well-equipped rooms on the second floor including a chapel and garderobe*

rectangular keeps were now joined on the landscape by towers of quatrefoil design. There were also cylinders, exemplified by Conisborough, Yorkshire, England, built for Hamelin (1180) in the French style of Villeneuve-sur-Yonne, as well as triangles and poly-gons. These experiments were being developed in turn, along with elements of systematic concentric defence such as the curtain wall and its interval towers, gatehouses, barbicans and water defences.

## THE RISE OF THE BARONS

Throughout Europe, royal families strove to extend their boundaries while also striving to curb the power of the barons. They, however, fought back to defend their freedom. The shape of towers changed and the curtain walls grew stron-ger, keeps began to disappear and to be replaced by a corner tower, or a massive gatehouse was used to serve the purpose.

Towards the end of the reign of Henry II, who succeeded in controlling the barons and the church alike by his policy of castle building, the keep at Dover was raised for the protec-tion of the narrow straights of Dover. It still stands today as a symbol of Angevin power.

## Dover Castle

Dover Castle is among the most important of all castles. It has the longest recorded history of any major fortress in Britain, and was seriously at risk only on one occasion. Its original rampart defences date from the prehistoric Iron Age. The

*Dover Castle is one of the oldest and most important. Perched high above the town on an ancient headland, it commands the historic gateway to England. The Castle has been in continuous military occupation for over 800 years. Its great tower, or keep, is one of the finest in England*

Romans built a pharos (light-house) on the site in the first century AD; they also built a second on the facing Western Heights. The site was resettled by the Anglo-Saxons who built a fortified town (burh) in the 10th century, of which St Mary in Castro was the church. Both the pharos and church still remain. The bulk of Dover Castle as we see it today dates from 100 years after the Norman Conquest. Although soon after the Battle of Hastings the conquering forces strengthened all the fortifications, none of this or the earlier work by Harold can be identified now. The great square keep was built by the Angevin King

**Above:** *the Castle entrance of the 1220s, 'Constable's Gate', the greatest gatehouse of its day. Comprising five towers, it projects forward over the moat to permit flanking fire along the walls. The quarters of the Constable were over the gate passage*

**Above right:** *the keep's only early entrance was up the steep steps of the forebuilding*

Henry II (1154-89) in the 1180s, together with the walls of the keeps surrounding the inner bailey and a stretch of the outer curtain wall towards the east. The remainder of the formid-able outer curtain, with the

orate keep entrance. A straight flight of stairs leads to the first-floor vestibule and up through an arch to the left. This was originally open to the sky, so commanded from the battlements above. Then you are confronted by a drawbridge, the pit of which still remains, followed by a third flight of stairs which ascend to the main residential floor of the keep. The second storey entrance is via a grand door leading into the upper vestibule. Hubert de Burgh was a veteran who had seen service since the reign of King Richard (*d* 1199). As Chief Justifier of England from 1215, de Burgh was responsible for the commissioning of castles. After the seige of Rochester, where the

gatehouses and the flanking towers, was erected under the direction of Hubert de Burgh (1203-32) under Henry III.

In the mid-eighteenth century the barracks were built and the defences remodelled. The keep is approached via a three-towered forebuilding, covering the keep's entry stairs and the two castle chapels. This building provides a most elab-

**Right:** *the polygonal Avranches Traverse at Dover, a purpose-built archery tower of the 1180s at the forefront of contemporary castle design. It has stacked fighting galleries and a bank of triple firing-loops, so distributed as to command the entire moat*

castle fell owing to the under-mining of the curtain towers surrounding the keep, and a similar experience at Dover when the outer gatehouse nearly fell to Prince Louis, his reaction was to strengthen all of Dover's other defences, giving less importance to the keep. In this way he trans-formed Dover into an offensive castle, pioneering the powerful residential gatehouse with its drawbridge, portcullis and long passage. Its towers projected forward over a steep-sided moat to permit flanking fire along the curtain.

His towers on the vulnerable northern quarter of the fortress were designed in the latest French fashion to resist being undermined, with sharp beak-shaped profiles. Other measures

**Previous pages:** *Dover's impressive layout; Constable's Gate is on the right, bottom left is the spur. Tracing back via the underground works are St John's Tower, and beyond the Norfolk Towers and the King's Gate just to the right of centre in front of the keep*

**Below:** *guns are still in place in the upper battery of the caponier. At the far end is the entrance to the bomb-proof underground passages and guardrooms of the redan*

**Right:** *the Peverell's Tower gatehouse has a big mural tower of King John's reign to the left, with a semi-circular tower to the right added in the 13th century. Its conical roof was probably added in about 1300*

to prevent the enemy coming too close included his unique system of underground works, each issuing at a sallyport. He made any besieging army more vulnerable than the garrison within, exposing it to assault at all times and from many different quarters.

Technical advances made to castle construction in England and France during the 12th century must have benefited from the crusaders' experience gained in the Holy Land and from the western seaboard of both the Byzantine and Islamic empires. Developments such as stone-built machicolated wall-walks and projecting galleries, complete with holes in the floor through which to drop missiles, were certainly to be found in the larger and more important royal buildings. The splayed wall bases (talus or glacis) helped to project missiles outwards when they were dropped through these machicolations, in addition to the extra strength they afforded the structure, and the added difficulty they presented to attackers trying to scale the walls. More important still was the siting of regularly-spaced flanking or mural towers, which had also been witnessed in Asia Minor. The advantage of these mural towers was greatly

to improve the fire-power of the garrison. (Dover Castle, with its 14 mural towers, of which four are gate towers, was Henry II's early exploitation of the system in the West.) These most certainly led to the ultimate decline of the traditional tower keep in favour of a concentric defence.

Richard I, once having experienced the Holy Land strongholds at first hand, retained the tower keep as the final strongpoint in building Château-Gaillard, Normandy, France, between 1196 and 1198. However, he also incorporated a strongly-splayed base, prominent machicolations, and three successive lines of defences crossing the site, and enclosing in turn an outer, a middle and an inner bailey. So arranged, the outer bailey was in effect a barbican, protected at its most vulnerable point by a great tower, circular in design and blocking the approaches to the middle bailey, the sole entrance to which was over a bridge that it controlled. Both the outer and the inner middle curtain walls had prominent drum towers to add further reinforcement. The inner curtain wall was finished off on the exterior with a completely individual series of large-scale corrugations which improved

*The early concentric design of Château-Gaillard embodied every new defensive concept known in the late 12th century*

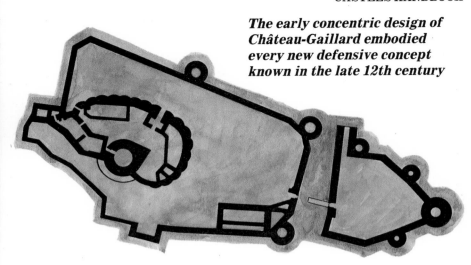

cover fire from the walkway. Early pioneering development of concentric defences and the refinement of the mural tower at Château-Gaillard were to become a benchmark for all future great castles.

As the royal castles became modernised, so they adopted these new fashions. Saumur was one of Philip Augustus' castles, built in the Roman manner, having a great tower at each of its four corners; while Angers was undoubtedly the most impressive, with its curtain wall that linked 17 drum towers. At the same time in England, Windsor, Dover and the Tower of London each had additional strong stone circuits built to add further to the defences, each with its lines of regularly-spaced towers.

*Château d'Angers, built on the site of the former fortress of Foulques. A pentagon some 660m (2,165ft) across, it is surrounded, except on the side overlooking the river, by 17 cylindrical towers, each 40-60m (131-197ft) high*

## Saumur and the châteaux of the Loire valley

Along the Loire, and along its hardly less celebrated tributaries, runs the royal road of 12th and 16th-century French monarchy. The history of France is visible everywhere, and especially in the many châteaux and palaces of the region.

Initially a duelling-ground, where the rivalries of the feuding earls of Blois and Anjou were given free rein until the 11th century, then an integral part of the kingdom of England under the 12th-century Plantegenets and the Capets until Philip Augustus was able finally to confiscate it from Jean 'The Landless' in the 13th century, the Loire valley was to become the Capets' main line of defence, notably under St Louis, its fortresses defending the bridges of the Loire against all lines of attack.

Under the Valois family in the 14th century and the Hundred Years' War, the whole situation of the Throne came into question in the succession to Charles VI. In 1429, with the appearance of Joan of Arc, the Kingdom of France was on the brink of ruin and elimination. Under Charles VII in the 15th century, royal legitimacy was

**Previous pages:** *the 15th-century fortress of Plessis-Bourré remains exactly as it was first built, without interruption, from 1468-73. It is the masterpiece of Jean Bourré. He also helped in building the Château of Langeais, so there is some similarity in concept between the two. Plessis-Bourré has a powerful cylindrical keep, crowned with a parapet and covered sentry walk, topped by another level set back from the rim, and the whole surmounted by a pepperpot turret*

**Above: *the barbican and fortified gatehouse of Montreuil-Bellay***

**Left: *Saumur, from the Duc de Berry's* Book of Hours**

restored, and until the 16th century the Loire valley became the seat of state of the royal court; a court which was still anguished by religious wars between 1560-98.

Under Henry IV, the first Bourbon King, the political and architectural decline of the châteaux set in, to be accentuated in the 17th century by the vengeance of Richelieu, followed by the reaction against the Fronde. The Revolution brought further destruction in the Consulate.

In the second half of the 14th century, Louis I of Anjou, brother of Charles V, built Saumur Castle as his country residence on the foundations of an earlier fortress. Its broad windows, elegant crenellated covered way and grand staircase with ornate openings give a foretaste of the Renaissance architecture to come.

The last Duke of Anjou, Good King René, described Saumur as a 'castle of love' in one of his 15th-century courtly romances. At the end of the 16th century, Saumur became a Protestant stronghold and its governor Duplessis Mornay, a

***General view of Saumur Castle from the south***

friend of Henri IV, took up residence in the castle. He hired an Italian engineer to build a surrounding wall, with redans and bastions. In the following years, the castle served as a residence for governors, gaol for noblemen imprisoned by order of the king's cachet and occasionally for prisoners of war. The building gradually decayed, and by the end of the 17th century the north-west wing was in ruins.

During the First Empire, it was converted first to become a State prison (the south-west wing has kept three floors of vaulted cells), subsequently to barracks, and then a military arsenal.

However, since the beginning of this century, the Castle has regained its original appearance so exquisitely illustrated in the *Book of Hours* belonging to the Duc de Berry. The drawbridge has disappeared but the bridgehead, flanked by two pepperpot turrets, still defends the entrance.

To gain access to the inner courtyard, you cross the guardroom with its original fireplace and barrel-vaulted porch protected by a portcullis.

The circular opening in the centre of the courtyard served

as an air-vent to the ancient water tank used in case of fire, its rainwater supply coming from the cistern still existing to the right of the hall door.

The 61m (200ft)-deep well has a 13th-century gear winch and one of the original dungeons still exists in the east tower. The grand staircase, *shown here from outside*, reaches three floors, which have crenellated windows each with openwork balustrades. At the top are the royal quarters.

As the 13th century progressed, so castle construction evolved, with greater impor-

**Overleaf:** *the Château from the north-east*

tance placed on the residential quality of the buildings of the inner ward. Upper floor levels gained larger windows and the private lodgings included larger rooms to accommodate growing numbers of guests, plus a division of rooms to provide more privacy for the lord. During modernisation, existing castles were also being converted to comfortable residences. Windsor, the Tower of London, Marlborough and Nottingham are a few examples of the upgraded castles with lodgings equipped for king and queen with their chapels, wardrobes and privy-chambers, new halls furnished to a higher standard and with improved roofing and flooring.

## HOME SWEET HOME

It is hard to imagine so many bleak ruins of medieval castles as once having been hospitable places, yet in their heyday they would have had wooden floor boards at every level, some laid over flagstones. Partitions would have provided some degree of privacy, while blazing fires provided both light and heat. Windows would have been glazed and curtained, and the thick hangings across doors would have prevented all but the worst draughts. The stone walls would have been both plastered and painted, and adorned with heraldic devices.

Sanitary and washing facilities existed, although of a primitive nature, and contrary to the popular image, dirty straw did not form the floor covering. If it was used for a feast, the straw would be clean, and after the event swept away by servants to leave the floorboards clean.

Each castle contained considerable stores of water, food and munitions. Fuel for heating and lighting, and fodder for livestock, had to be carefully housed in storerooms, some fitted out with shelves and racks in cool, dry conditions.

Although prison cells or dungeons existed in the medieval castles, their function was primarily only for the temporary incarceration of retainers or soldiers guilty of breaking a garrison rule. Any rebellious peasants could more easily be publicly flogged, rather than locked up, when perforce they must be fed; the prince held for ransom would have had to have been kept in good health and was therefore more likely to be confined to a residential part of the castle.

*Windsor Castle, a royal residence for over 900 years*

## EDWARD'S WELSH DEFENCES

Harlech Castle in Gwynedd, Wales, was built in the summer months of 1283-89 by an army of 1,000 labourers made up of volunteers, contractors and pressed men from all over the kingdom. One of Edward I's great chain of fortresses, now regarded as seminal in castle-building in the West, planning it as a concentric castle allowed the inner defenders to fire over the heads of men on the outer walls.

The man in charge of the new castles in North Wales was Master James of St George, who, when the work was completed, was appointed as the Constable of Harlech, a post he held until 1293.

The castles with which Edward enforced the English settlement in North Wales combined as standard the regularly-spaced mural towers, successfully employed at Dover over a century before, with the double enclosure and geometric plan. Both of the latter have their origins in antiquity, and were employed in the Holy Land by the times of the Crusades. The Edwardian fortress also featured an almost-impregnable gatehouse, such as that which Hubert de Burgh had constructed at Dover, and seen so effective in the great Hospitaller castle at Krak des Chevaliers, in Syria.

Edward's castles must be considered as a whole, the major ones being at Flint and Rhuddlan (1277), Conwy, Caernarfon and Harlech (1283) and Beaumaris (1295). A series of ten buildings in all, possible only because of the available investment, and focusing the latest in military engineering in an attempt to pacify Wales.

### MEN OF HARLECH

Harlech Castle has been besieged five times since it was built, firstly in 1294, when 37 men had defended the Castle against Prince Madoc, who was finally forced to abandon his seige when relief for the Castle arrived by sea. Harlech did succumb over a century later, when the fortress, no longer in good repair, was surrendered to Owain Glyndwr following his three-year seige, only for a 1,000-strong Anglo-Norman force to retake the Castle in 1409 from a starving garrison.

Flint demonstrates the French influence on Edward's castles, with its tower keep in

***Plans of Edward's six Welsh castles***

FLINT

RHUDDLAN

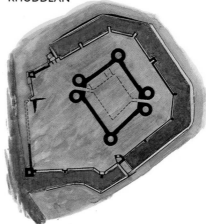

CONWY

HARLECH

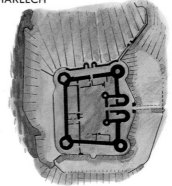

CAERNARFON

BEAUMARIS

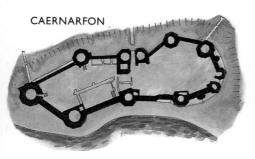

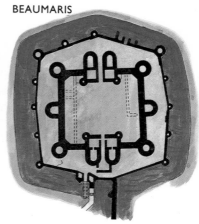

the south-east corner of the inner bailey, surrounded by a moat, and providing the main residential accommodation.

Flint, like Rhuddlan, was associated with purpose-built towns, planted in North Wales and Gascony, to build up units of permanent settlement that were intended to be more viable than a fortress on its own.

## Beaumaris Castle

Begun in 1295, it was the last and the largest of King Edward I's Welsh castles. Designed by Master James of St George, Beaumaris *above right* is the ultimate in symmetrical concentric design. Surrounded by a water-filled moat and with its own protected access to the sea, it had its own medieval docks capable of handling ships of 40 tonnes (88,184lb). The concentric castle, with one high ring of defence inside a lower one, was first perfected at Caerphilly in 1268, and had advantages of economy, unity and compactness over the older keep and bailey castle system. It also afforded a tremendous increase in fire power with the second line of defences able to fire over the outer walls.

The Castle features a 5.5m (18ft) moat, which originally encircled it, and also an octa-gonal outer curtain wall with 16 towers; unhappily, Beaumaris was never completed owing to lack of finances.

## Caernarfon Castle

The last great castle of King Edward I's second Welsh campaign, Caernarfon *below right* was built mostly from 1283–92, though additional work did continue until 1323, following the sacking by the Welsh in 1294. A fortress palace, it was designed as the new seat of government for North Wales, and was the birthplace of Edward II in 1284. Caernarfon withstood the assaults of Owain Glyndwr, defended by a garrison of only 28 men, but was surrendered in the Civil War. The Castle was extensively restored in Victorian and later times, and was the site of the ceremonial investiture of Prince Charles as the Prince of Wales in July 1969. The Castle has been owned continuously by the Crown. Its plan is quite unusual, being shaped rather like an hourglass which was originally divided by a cross-wall at the narrowest part into two wards. The earthen mound of an earlier Norman motte and bailey castle, built in 1090 by Earl Hugh of Chester, occupies most of the upper ward.

## INFLUENCE OF THE WELSH CASTLES

Beaumaris is without doubt a classic of its kind, a triumph in design that had almost bankrupted Edward's kingdom. It was without any doubt revered throughout Europe as a notable step forward in the science of fortification, and was copied as far as was possible at Villandraut, Guyenne, France, an early 14th-century castle built for Clement V, the first French Pope, at Avignon; others inspired by Edward's successes were Hanstein in Germany, Marschlins in Switzerland and Muiden in the Netherlands. Another castle where design must be considered as being well-thought out and definitely taking advantage of modern thinking was the castle at Caerlaverock, Dumfriesshire, Scotland.

This was built in about 1270, to a triangular plan, and has an extremely impressive double-towered keep-gatehouse at the apex together with prominent drum towers at each of its other two angles. A water-filled moat surrounds it, contained by an earth rampart, which together form an outer line of defence. Caerlaverock displays all of the design features embodied in Edward's castles, which had evolved to their climax of sophistication over a generation of continuous fortress-building in Wales. The main points of these are:

- a rigid geometric plan
- concentric defences
- effective angle tower
- highly-fortified gatehouse
- main residence in gatehouse

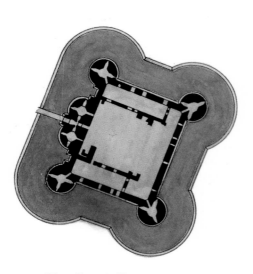

***Villandraut, France, was influenced by Edwardian castle building* see page 41**

Exceptional gatehouses of the period can be seen today at Rockingham (Northamptonshire, England) and Tonbridge (Kent, England).

**Above and below:** *Caerlaverock Castle was built in the 1270s by Sir Herbert de Maxwell with a twin-towered gatehouse and keep combined around the entrance. It is still a most beautiful castle, and features a grand stairway to the rooms on the eastern flank*

**Overleaf:** *Rockingham Castle was built by William the Conqueror on the site of an earlier fortification. It was a royal fortress used by the early kings of England until the 16th century, when it was granted by Henry VIII to Edward Watson, whose descendants still live there. The Castle walls are Norman, although the dominant influence in the building is Tudor*

# STRONGHOLDS OF THE INFIDELS

When Rome was overrun by the Goths in 410, the architects of the Byzantine Emperor Theodosius II improved the defences of Constantinople by means of building concentric fortifications on the landward side of the city. First a 38m (124ft 8in) wide ditch was proposed, 6.5m (21ft 4in) deep, flooded with water, with the bottom of the ditch spiked. Inside the ditch, a 5.5m (18ft) high wall was to be 2m (6ft 6.7in) thick, with at every 55m (180ft 5.5in) a projecting tower sited to provide flanking fire. A third wall provided the next line of defence, 4.5m (14ft 9in) thick and 27m (88ft 7in) high, faced with stone and reinforced with courses of brick. This wall also had projecting towers along its length, sited so that their field of fire was not obscured by the outer bastions. From them, catapult artillery were employed.

The whole system was tiered, so that the men on the higher inner walkways could fire over the heads of their brothers in arms who manned the outer defences.

In addition to the land-based defences of Constantinople, the Byzantine emperors controlled vast fleets and armies, which

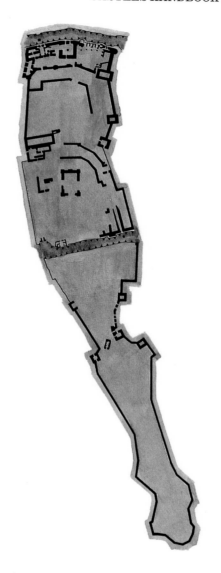

***Sahyan,** above, **was influenced by pre-existing Byzantine defences***

47

ranged from the Mediterranean to the Middle East, keeping their enemies at bay. They also gained a reputation for terrible oppression and so were much hated. Knowing this, they had prepared themselves for the inevitable attack. There were attempts to usurp this vast empire, which extended from India to the Atlantic and from France to the Equator. Vikings from the north, Romanised barbarians from the west, Mongols from the east, and from 622 the Arabs from the south all tried. Yet the city of Constantinople stood firm, repelling two seiges in 655 by Muslims. The latter argued among themselves, and despite being able to launch a direct assault on the walls from the sea, by 675 they had lost over 30,000 men and retreated.

In 717, the Saracens returned by both land and sea to mount an effective blockade, and the Byzantines had resorted to cannibalism before an army from Christian Bulgaria inflicted devastating defeats on the Saracens, forcing them to retreat.

The leaders of the Fourth Crusade were persuaded by the Venetian rich to overthrow the walls of Constantinople. Successful in their attempts, the Crusaders waited patiently for the Venetians who had taken up

residence to pay their dues. The Crusaders assaulted the city again in 1204, from both land and water, breaching the walls and plundering the city; they then established one of their own as Emperor Baldwin I.

Constantinople remained the capital of a Latin empire until 1261, when Michael VIII Palaeologus took possession of the city for the Orthodox faith.

## FIRE POWER

Once more the city changed hands, in 1453; the major contributing factor to its downfall was gunpowder and cannon.

Inevitably gunpowder and cannon improved over the years of the 15th century, and their most spectacular success was achieved at Constantinople. The city had been beseiged for just two months in 1422 during the Turkish invasion of Europe, but because of heavy losses inflicted upon the Ottomans and troubles in other parts of their kingdom they desisted, only to return 31 years later. The Great Seige began on 6 April 1453, when 60,000 Turks surrounded Constantinople. The 7,000 Byzantine defenders were well stocked with food and water and were confident that as before they could hold out.

The Ottomans applied their

cannon to the task, which were still unreliable and apt to overheat or even burst; they were able to average only seven rounds a day, fired in rotation. They were concentrated on the very weakest parts of the defensive land walls.

The first breaches were made on the twelfth day, 18 April, but were firmly repulsed. Having retreated to consider the situation Mehmet II, the Ottoman leader, decided on a marine approach. Constantinople had been successfully defended previously by blocking both the Dardanelles and the Bosphorus. Protecting the city were a series of booms, chains and blocking ships across the entrance to the Golden Horn, but this time the Byzantine fleet was not in control. Mehmet II ordered a road to be built around Galata, which formed the fortifications on the shore opposite Constantinople itself. The road was some 8km (4.97 miles) in length, and the Ottoman fleet was dragged down it on greased rollers and launched into the Golden Horn. A three-pronged attack now ensued on 29 May from the landward side, the Sea of Marmara and from the Golden Horn. At first the onslaught failed and it was not until a secret tunnel was discovered under the city walls that Constantinople was doomed.

**Below:** *Rambures, Picardy, France, was built in the mid-15th century. It was a tower-house of the early artillery age and incorporated gun-ports. The construction was in brick, with some of the finer detail in stone*

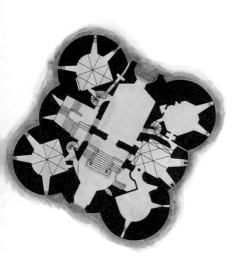

*Depicted overleaf is the artillery fort of Salses, Roussillon, France, a late-15th century pioneering construction which was later modified to remove some of the smaller turrets which were considered unsafe and more vulnerable, with the advent of increased artillery power*

## MOBILE ARTILLERY

The primitive bombards of the Turks were long outdated by the end of the 15th century, when Charles VIII of France introduced the wheeled artillery weapon, both lighter and with a higher muzzle velocity; these also had barrels that could depress or elevate.

The advent of gunpowder had also brought with it the mine, which was originally a keg of gunpowder placed in a mine under the fortress walls and detonated to blast a way through the solid foundations. The explosive device, rather than the tunnel in which it was placed, took the name mine.

Another form of explosive mine was the petard, used above ground. This was a con-tainer of gunpowder, placed against the wall by some unfortunate soldier who then had to light the fuse before hurrying away. Should the fuse be too long, the defenders could extinguish it with water; too short, and the soldier never returned: hence the expression, hoist by his own petard.

Another weapon developed at the same time was the high-trajectory mortar. A short fat cannon was used for lobbing the missile over the highest walls, but the early stone cannonballs shattered on impact. The new iron cannonballs buried themselves as they landed. The first successful mortars were explosive shells, ignited before firing. Castles, for all their defences, were being rendered unsafe.

## HENRY, DEFENDER OF THE FAITH

In 1538 the Pope excommunicated Henry VIII, and Charles V and Francis I (King of France) joined forces and prepared to invade England. Henry VIII in readiness ordered the construction of a series of castles to dominate the sea approaches and protect the most vulnerable harbours. By now, the accepted cannon range was 5km (3 miles), the extent of territorial waters, so these castles would dominate the coasts.

Henry's coastal forts provided living quarters first and foremost for soldiers, not lords or kings. The emergent castle in plan form has often been compared to a Tudor rose, and these were not unlike those of the German expert Haschenberg in both plan or elevation. They comprised a central stone building containing a spiral stone staircase leading from the basement to the top floor, which was covered by a cupola. At night, candle-lanterns set behind irremovable glass and only accessed by a separate corridor provided light for the staircase, as well as the depths of the fortress where the gunpowder was stored.

The spiral staircase was the central axis of the round tower

*Henry VIII's artillery fort at St Mawes which stands opposite Falmouth, Devon, was built between 1540 and 1543. The highest tower above is shown in the centre of the original plan below*

which comprised the basement, ground floor, upper floor and roof. Such was the solid construction that all upper-level floors carried cannon, the muzzles of which projected through embrasures in the walls. Battlements were also thicker than their medieval counterparts, and often were rounded vertically to deflect cannonballs up and over the roof gunners' heads.

This central tower was surrounded by six semicircular bastions, lower than the central tower but built the same way with access to the tower at first and ground floor levels. Cannon were mounted upon the roofs of the six bastions while their lower level afforded musketeers space to fire at anybody attempting an approach.

A further ring of six outlying bastions was joined in a circle connected to the inner bastions by underground tunnels. Outside, a wide and deep artificial ditch covered by musket ports from the outer ring of bastions provided a further obstacle, and the ditch itself was surrounded by a low wall. A single entrance existed via a drawbridge, which spanned the ditch and led to one of the outer bastions through strong doors, and a portcullis, both of which were repeated again between the bastions and the central building.

These new forts were constructed by Henry at Sandown, Deal, Walmer and Sandgate along the Kent coast, at Calshot and Hurst on the Solent, and at Portland in Devon. Existing fortifications at Dover and Camber were expanded, and by 1540 Henry VIII was ready. In the event the invasion never transpired, but Henry continued fortify west and north around the coast, including the erection of blockhouses.

By 1543, Henry had transferred his liking for the German Haschenberg's round compact castle to mainstream Italian fortress design, like that built at Southsea. This has a square keep inside a square bailey, but at right angles with its entrance. North and south curtain walls thereby formed angle bastions, the east and west corners being formed into gun platforms also rectangular in shape, and built of sufficiently solid earth to mount heavy cannon. The whole of the complex was surrounded by a dry ditch.

In 1545, the French invasion was aborted but Henry, Mary Tudor and Elizabeth I continued to develop fortifications based on the vee-shaped or arrowhead bastions.

### Cahir Castle

*An aerial view of Cahir Castle*

Larger and more complex than most Irish castles, Cahir's plan was dictated by the island in the Suir on which it stands.

The site is divided into outer, middle and inner wards. The original castle, which was built in the 13th century, is confined to the inner ward area, the highest and most commanding part of the site. The very thick curtain walls of the north and east sides of the ward and the massive wall-footing running west of the well tower and the outer wall of the hall of the west

side of the ward show the outline of the original fortress. In its final evolved state, the fortress represented a formidable problem for any assailant. The outer curtain formed a reasonably strong wall, with a walkway on top and two circular towers at the southern end. Beyond that, are the middle wall, which overlooks the outer ward, and the final defences comprising the keep with the portcullis barring entry into the inner ward. The keep and the towers at the north-west

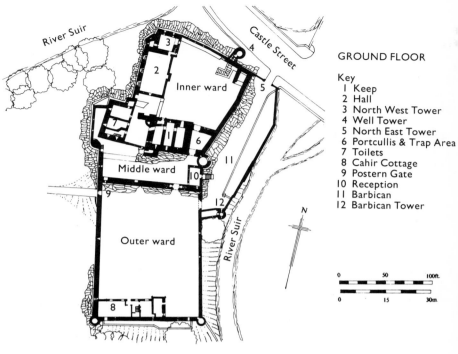

Key
1  Keep
2  Hall
3  North West Tower
4  Well Tower
5  North East Tower
6  Portcullis & Trap Area
7  Toilets
8  Cahir Cottage
9  Postern Gate
10 Reception
11 Barbican
12 Barbican Tower

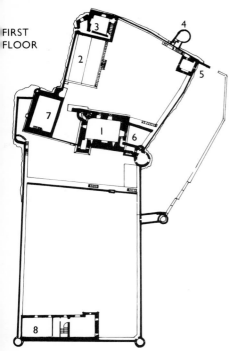

FIRST FLOOR

Key
1 Keep
2 Hall
3 North West Tower
4 Well Tower
5 North East Tower
6 Portcullis & Trap Area
7 Toilets
8 Cahir Cottage

SECOND FLOOR

**Above left and right:**
*Cahir visitors' plan today*

and north-east corners were capable of independent defence. The high rock foundations protected the Castle from attack by battering ram or by mining and so Cahir, prior to the advent of the cannon, was a well thought-out castle that could be properly defended by a well-armed garrison.

In 1599, Queen Elizabeth I sent the Earl of Essex to Ireland with an army of almost 18,000 men to defeat the rebellion headed by Tyrone. On 23 May the garrison at Cahir, under the command of James Gallda Butler, refused an offer to sur-

render. Essex with 3,000 foot soldiers laid seige to the Castle.

Essex had a cannon and a culverin, which had been dragged to Cahir by the English soldiers from Clonmel. Neither cannon nor culverin was reliable, both often breaking down, but by the third day of the assault, 28 May, the east wall was breached and the Castle taken with the loss of about 80 defenders' lives.

The capture of Cahir was of little significance to the Irish campaign, but shows how a castle that was earlier near-impregnable would succumb quickly to light artillery fire.

*Cahir Castle and the River Suir*

**Overleaf:** *the Keep*

## Schönburg Castle

Near Oberwesel on the Rhine, it was probably first built in the 10th century, and was once described by Victor Hugo as 'one of the most venerable hills of rubble of all Europe'. There is a reference in 1166 to an old tower (maybe the northern tower, in ruins since 1880), a new tower (perhaps the massive gate tower which still remains) and a tower under construction. In the 14th century the Castle was co-hereditary, with this largest of Rhenish holdings home to three families, with up to 250 inhabitants sharing well-equipped accommodations.

In March 1689, the town of Oberwesel was fired by 1,600 French soldiers billeted there, destroying the hospital, the town hall, Schönburg manor, and 117 houses. At this time, Friedrich von Schönburg was killed fighting for the English at the Battle of the Boyne.

The Castle remained a ruin for two centuries. Rebuilding was begun at the beginning of the 20th century by an American, Mr Rhinelander. His son sold the newly-restored Castle to the town council of Oberwesel.

An inventory made in 1596 of Schönburg's arms reads as follows:

14 swords and rapiers
2 holsters for heavy rider's gun bullets
1 Turkish sabre
4 white armours and 6 helmets to match
7 black armours and 25 black headpieces
4 spears
16 lances
9 double hooks [heavy firearms that had to be placed on a jack in order to be operated]
17 small firearms, partly with match lock and partly with flint locks
5 pistols
1 regimental staff
several crossbows
2 hammers
5 mail shirts with sleeves
1 club with nails [called a *morgenstern* or morningstar]
1 black and white signal horn
1 small brass gun
3 short iron mortars
1 silken flag (white, yellow, blue) with Kurpflaz ensign
1 long lance
7 long-barreled rifles
7 pistols
170 finely-wrought scabbards
150 muskets
200 pikes
113 armours for infantrymen
109 iron collars
209 headpieces
3 complete knight's armours

2 shot-proof armours for infantrymen
4 drums
1 rider's flag with stick
5 guns of metal
15 horses
1 mule

**Left: *Schönburg Castle is now owned by the town council of Oberwesel***

## Castel Beséno

Two Italian castle engineers of the 15th century, Filippo Brunelleschi and Francisco de Giorgio, had reintroduced the idea of the bastion projecting from the curtain wall or from the corners to fire on any assailants who had made their way to the base of the adjacent bastion walls. However, unlike most of the earlier medieval towers, their bastions were usually of the same height or lower than the curtain wall, plus a caponier of even lower profile, in effect no more than a fortified corridor room at right angles across a dry ditch, so that the defenders could fire on any of the enemy at the base of the walls.

Castel Beséno in the province of Trento, Italy, is a fortified and turreted castle, and covers an entire hilltop, which makes it able to control the road below which leads to the province of Vincenza.

In all, it covers an area of 16,400m$^2$ (19,614.4sq yd), and is one of the largest castles on the southern side of the central Alps. The 15th-century fortifications which resulted from the introduction of firearms remain as three majestic keeps and their small yards for cannon. The tournament field, the traps, and the elegant Filandèla loggia are proof of its eventful past. The two castle walls enclose the three medieval nuclei enfeoffed by the Lords of Beséno. Following a feud of the Prince-Bishops at the beginning of the 14th century, the Castle remained the property of the Castelbarco family, until the second half of the next century, when it was bought by the Trapp family.

The 17th century was the era of the non-royal generals, of specialists who played at warfare like a game of chess across Europe. One such specialist in military architecture was the Dutch Baron Mennoe van Loehorn (1641-1704), who developed the new counterscarp gallery, located in the reverse slope of a dry moat and usually only accessible from the keep by underground tunnel. This enabled fire to be brought upon attackers who had got into the ditch. Others included his fellow-countryman Sir Bernard de Gomme (1620-1685) and, much earlier, Francesco Paciotto d'Urbino. He had been responsible for the citadel at Antwerpen.

## Sebastien le Prestre de Vauban

The greatest was Sebastien le Prestre de Vauban (1633-1707), marshal of France under Louis XIV and the greatest military engineer of the early modern period and also the undisputed master of seige warfare. During a career that extended from the Fronde until the War of the

*Now beautifully restored, Castel Beséno belongs to the Province of Trento and is one of the largest castles on the southern side of the Alps. The 15th-century fortification plan was the result of the introduction of firearms*

Spanish Succession, he had developed a theory and practice of seigecraft and fortification which served as the model for warfare until the Napoleonic era.

Vauban wrote a manual for young military engineers, outlining step-by-step the proper conduct for seiges and defences in which he detailed the following table for the setting up of mortar batteries, 'their range being at best 280 yards':

**Number of cannon:** 16
**Length of battery:** 98 yds (118 paces)
**Soldiers for construction:** 190
**Soldiers to make fascines and stakes, each with a knife and axe:** 85
**Other varied tools:** 280
**Fascines, 8–9ft long and 8–9in thick:** 750
    **12ft long and 8–9in thick for embrasures:** 320
    **5–6ft long and 5–6in thick:** 1,600
**Stakes 3–6ft long 1½–3in thick on top:** 3,600
**Sledgehammers to drive stakes:** 66
**Knives for the embrasures:** 32
**Timbers 2–2½in thick for platforms:** 256
**Men to serve the guns:** 32
**Soldiers to supply the guns:** 96
**Powder for a day's firing, firing 100 rounds each, using 12lb charge:** 19,200lbs
**24lb ball for day's firing:** 1,600

Vauban was the architect whose evolutionary effect upon warfare was to bring to it discipline and planning. The French Army's seige operations were conducted under his direction. He co-ordinated bombardment of all the individual batteries, and deliberately employed ricochet fire to reach targets positioned between ramparts. He introduced the systematic application of use of trenches, employed at the successful seige of Maastricht in 1673 that took just 13 days.

Vauban also spent much of his time in the rebuilding of the French fortresses, to bring them up to a standard that could successfully withstand the type of seige operation which he himself would use. It is claimed that no fewer than 150 citadelled towns owe their defences to Vauban, the last of the influential castle builders and destroyers.

**Overleaf:** *view of Leeds Castle, from where the inner barbican stood in medieval times, looking towards the main gate of the castle c 1280. Runnels for the portcullis and a recess for the drawbridge still exist*

## Leeds Castle

According to legend, the local thane of Eslder (Leeds) built a fort on top of a rocky outcrop in the valley of the River Lea. Although no trace remains, it is known that the Manor of Leeds was a possession of the Saxon royal line, probably as early as the middle of the 9th century, at about the time of the reign of Ethelbert IV (856-866).

Just prior to the Conquest, King Edward the Confessor had granted the Manor to the house of Godwin. After the Conquest, in 1090, William II (Rufus) granted Leeds to his cousin, Hamm de Crèvecoeur, as a reward for his part in the Battle of Hastings.

Robert de Crèvecoeur began work on a stone castle on the site in 1119, establishing his keep and incorporating an existing mill that stood on the brink of the river into the defences at the outer gate.

It is thought that a drawbridge connected the fortified mill to the inner gatehouse, with the Castle standing astride the River Lea and including two islands, the larger of which was surrounded by walls up to 15.25m (50ft)

**Right:** *the Castle as viewed from the north-east; behind the medieval gloriette is the Georgian house*

**Overleaf:** *a view of the main Castle with the gloriette in the background*

inside the revetment wall. The domestic buildings were all located at the northern end of the bailey and connected to the keep or gloriette by a drawbridge over the water-filled ditch. The principal apartment of the keep was the hall, which occupied much of the west side.

Henry I died in 1135, leaving the Crown contested between Stephen and his cousin the Empress Matilda, who invaded England in 1139 with the help of her brother Robert, Earl of Gloucester. Leeds Castle was held by the Earl of Gloucester, but following a short seige by the loyal men of Kent, the Castle soon fell to King Stephen.

The Castle was yielded by Robert de Crèvecoeur, who was a great-great-grandson of the Castle's builder, to Sir Roger de Leyburn, a friend and supporter of Henry III against whom de Crèvecoeur had fought at the Battle of Lewes in 1264.

In 1278, Lord William de Leyburn, the son of Sir Roger, conveyed Leeds Castle to King Edward and Queen Elinor. Both King and Queen used the Castle extensively, both enjoying it themselves and entertaining, especially continental dignitaries, as Edward's mother was Eleanor of Provence.

**Left: *the bridge corridor linking the two parts of the Castle dates from 1822***

**Right: *the 16th-century newel staircase, built entirely in oak, provides access to the first floor at the end of the Castle. The central fluted newel post was carved from a single tree trunk***

Extensive alterations were made by Edward I, perfecting the embankments that surrounded the moat, which was now a lake protected by a dam. This Edward further protected by building a barbican which was connected both to the mill and to the gatehouse.

The wall around the larger island was also strengthened by the addition of **D**-shaped turrets, with the upper storeys loop-holed for the archers' use. The gatehouse too was extended to the edge of the revetment wall, which afforded greater protection to both the dam and the barbican.

The Constable's quarters were sited within the gatehouse, with the Castle guards. The guardhouse commanded the three approach roads, all of which had to cross narrow causeways.

**Above: *the picturesque Castle provides a panorama of architecture from the twelfth to the twentieth century***

**Right: *the Fountain Court, the central courtyard of the gloriette, dates from the 1280s. In the 14th century, a system was devised to bring water in pipes from the springs in the park into cisterns beneath the paving to supply the fountains. The same springs supply the Castle today***

Queen Elinor died in 1290, and in 1299 Edward married Margaret, the sister of Philip III of France, and granted the Castle to his new Queen. Edward II granted the Castle to Lord Bartholomew de Badlesmere, unbeknown to his own Queen Isabella who, in 1321, sought shelter for the night at Leeds Castle and was refused, the Castle guard firing upon the royal party and killing several of the Queen's guards. Edward, in retaliation, beseiged the Castle, which he captured. Lord Bartholomew's fate was to be beheaded. Following the later murder of Edward II in 1327, Parliament granted the Castle to Queen Isabella again.

Leeds Castle was enlarged under Edward III, and repaired by Henry IV, including the renewal of drawbridge to the great tower. In later years, Queen Joan, wife of Henry V, and Eleanor Cobham, Duchess of Gloucester, King Henry VI's aunt, were both imprisoned at the Castle.

Henry VIII made the most important alterations to Leeds since those made by Edward III. He transformed the great tower, superimposing canted bay windows of 16 lights in the royal apartments and repaired all of the royal rooms. The Maiden's Tower was reconstructed.

**Below: *the small yet comfortable Queen's Bedroom, and right the Queen's Bathroom, both prepared as they may have been for Catherine de Valois in the year 1430***

## SOME CASTLES TO VISIT

Alnwick Castle, *above*, is a magnificent border fortress, the second largest inhabited castle in England. It dates back to the 11th century and had been in the possession of the Percys, Earls and Dukes of Northumberland, since 1309. It was erected by Yvo de Vessey, the first Norman Baron of Alnwick, who became the owner soon after 1066. The mighty stronghold now lies in a peaceful landscape designed by 'Capability' Brown, and was restored to its present splendour by the fourth Duke between 1854 and 1865.

The internal decoration is in the classical Italian Renaissance style, which has replaced the Gothic decoration carried out by Robert Adam in the 18th century. The Castle has some of the finest examples of Italian paintings in the north of England, works by van Dyck and Turner, an excellent collection of early Meissen porcelain and the regimental museum of the Royal Northumberland Fusiliers in the Abbot's Tower.

Arundel Castle, *right,* lies just 29km (18 miles) west of Brighton and was built at the end of the 11th century by Roger de Montgomery, Earl of Arundel. This great castle has been the seat of the Dukes of Norfolk and their ancestors for over 700 years.

It was extensively damaged in 1643 during the Civil War, when bombarded by the Parliamentary forces, and during its subsequent occupation. It was largely rebuilt in the 18th century and two further towers were added in the late 18th century.

Inside, the Castle is rich in art treasures, including works by van Dyck, Gainsborough and Reynolds; the Baron's Hall is a splendid reproduction medieval hall. The library, built early in the 19th century, measures $35.66 \times 10.66$m $(117 \times 35$ft) and is constructed entirely of Honduras mahogany.

England's oldest inhabited castle, Berkeley Castle *below* was completed in 1153 at the command of Henry II. A magnificent stately home full of treasures has been created by 24 generations of Berkeleys.

In 1215, the West Country barons met there before travelling to Runnymede so as to force King John to sign *Magna Carta*; in 1327, Edward II was murdered in the dungeon cell.

Berkeley Landing in Virginia, now the oldest working plantation in America, was established by the 38 Berkeley men who sailed from Bristol in 1619, and who held the very first Thanksgiving there on 4 December 1619.

Bodelwydden Castle, Clwyd, Wales, *right* is 50km (31 miles) west of Liverpool, and stands on a site which has been inhabited since 1460. Purchased by Sir William Williams, Speaker of the House of Commons, in 1680, the Castle underwent extensive alterations under the first baronet of Bodelwydden at the beginning of the 19th century. The present gothic appearance is the result of work carried out by his son, Sir John Hay-Williams, in the 1830s when the towers were created and the battlements added to the parapet.

In 1982, the Castle was acquired by Clwyd County Council. In partnership with the National Portrait Gallery, it has since redecorated and refurbished the principal rooms.

Donegal Castle, Co Donegal, Ireland *below* stands on a site where a castle has been since the 12th century. The original castle built by the O'Donnells was burnt in 1159 by Murtogh McLoughlin. Hugh Roe O'Donnell erected a new one in 1477, and in 1611 this in turn was granted to Captain Basil Brooke.

Brooke had gone to Ireland in 1598 with the English Army, fought in Munster, and was appointed a servitor of the Ulster Plantation. During the later rebellion of 1641, Donegal Castle was held by Sir Basil's heir, Henry Brooke, though Clanrickarde took it for a short period in 1651. Henry Brooke subsequently resided there. It fell into decay in the 18th century and the owner, the Earl of Arran, placed the Castle in the guardianship of the Office of Public Works.

The Castle of Olité in Navarra, Spain, *right* and *far right* lies 42km (28 miles) south of Pamplona and is one of the most Gothic civil works in Europe. This royal palace was built on the site of a Roman praesidium, and has been modified several times. It was the home of Navarrese kings during the 13th and 14th centuries, the most notable of whom, Charles III of Navarra, restored the old Palace and built its large towers which still survive.

The picturesque complexity of its plan has no equal among other buildings of its type. A diverse and secretive castle, Olité is said to have as many rooms as there are days in the year, which are linked by countless galleries and winding stairs, each successive room being more sumptuous than the one before it.

Eilean Donan, Scotland *below* is located 108km (67 miles) north-west of Fort William, standing on the island of St Donan in Loch Duish. It is linked to the mainland by a bridge.

The Castle was reconstructed earlier in this century, and restored as the headquarters of the Clan MacRae. Originally the home of the hermit St Donan, the island was given to Colin Fitzgerald in the 13th century, when the Castle was a plain walled enclosure. Eilean Donan passed from the Crown to the Mackenzies, then to the MacDonalds, and then to the MacRaes in 1506. In 1719, three British frigates attacked the Castle, their cannon soon destroying Eilean Donan, which remained an overgrown ruin until rebuilt in replica by Lt Col John MacRae-Gilstrop.

The original Castle, with its 14th-century keep, was not well fortified; today's banqueting hall is where the great hall once stood. This is well furnished with historical knicknacks and fine furniture and a magnificent wrought iron yett (hinged grille), recovered from the well at the time of the restoration.

Fyvie Castle, in Grampian Region, Scotland, is located 38km (24 miles) north of Aberdeen and is built on the site of a large medieval castle. The original royal stronghold with walls 2.5m (98in) thick and 8m (26ft 3in) high passed into the hands of Sir James de Linsay in 1380. The Castle, *illustrated above*, forms a figure 2, with the medieval walls forming the base and upright; the upper part, Leith Tower, was added in the 19th century. The Castle was transformed by Lord Fyvie, the first Earl of Dunfermline and Chancellor of Scotland, in 1601. This includes the celebrated southern façade, which joined the Edwardian gatehouse and the linking curtain wall to the eastern and western towers. Its wheeled stair remains the finest in Scotland, and the 17th-century morning room was by the first Lord Leith.

At the end of the 17th century, the Castle had fallen into disrepair but was purchased by William Gordon. A new northern tower was built, and the surrounding marshes drained. Today, the Castle features some beautiful plasterwork and panelling, armour and weaponry, plus the famous Green Lady ghost. It stands in 47.75ha (118 acres) of parkland.

Inveraray Castle, Strathclyde, Scotland, lies just 60km (37 miles) north-west of Glasgow and is the home of the Dukes of Argyll and headquarters of the Campbell clan.

The Castle *illustrated below* and the small town, which lie along the banks of Loch Fyne, were the brainchild of the third Duke, Archibald Campbell, and were first built in the middle of the 18th century. An original concept by Vanbrugh, the Castle as seen today is primarily the work of Roger Morris, who was assisted by William Adam and his sons John and Robert.

The classic interior was arranged by Robert Mylne. The rectangular Castle features a State Dining Room, which has painted wall panels and a Robert Adam-designed ceiling; the very elaborate Tapestry Drawing Room has Beauvais tapestries. There is also an Armoury Hall.

The Roman keep of Loches, France, is a rectangular mass 37m (121ft 5in) in height. In the 11th century, it was reinforced by a ring of semicircular buttresses, the four stories of which are lit only by narrow firing slits. Movement from floor to floor was by means of stairways buried in the thickness of the walls. This formidable, impregnable stronghold was built by Foulques Nerra, the Count of Anjou, before 1041, and can still be seen today *illustrated right* in its awesome beauty.

It stands roofless between the new tower and the martelet, both of which date from the fifteenth century. All three are within the 13th-century fortification, to which were added three impressive towers, sharp-edged like the bars of a ship, built by Philip Augustus.

Peckforton Castle is located about 40km (25 miles) south of Liverpool. Built by John Tollemach, Member of Parliament of Cheshire between 1841 and 1872, the Castle *above* was constructed in stone from a quarry a mile away. The architect was Anthony Salvin, who created a functional Victorian home in the style of a 12th-century castle, which is approached through a forbidding gatehouse with its giant archway and broad battlements.

The Castle features a chapel with a hexagonal bell turret, stables, coach house, kitchen and servants' wing, which are grouped around a small courtyard; also the Great Hall with a high stone-vaulted ceiling, an ornate carved screen and minstrels' gallery. The unique octagonal dining room rests on a cave-like wine cellar. First opened to the public in 1990, the Castle was the venue in 1991 where Twentieth-Century Fox filmed *Robin Hood.*

Ripley Castle in North Yorkshire, England, *right* has been the home of the Ingilbys for more than 660 years. The fortified gatehouse dates from the 1450s; the Old Tower, which houses the library of over 2,500 books, dates from 1555.

In 1603, the future King James I stayed there, prompting the building of the magnificent plaster ceiling in the Tower Room. A Georgian wing was added in 1782/3. The Knight's Chamber has the original 1555 wood panelling and waggon roof ceiling. A priest's hiding hole, only discovered by accident in 1964, was actually made in 1584.

# GLOSSARY

**Aisled:** divided into three parts longitudinally by two arcades supporting the roof

**Allure:** the wall-walk which runs behind the battlements

**Apse:** the rounded east wall of a church or chapel

**Arcade:** a row of arches; when applied to a wall and used for decorative purposes, **blind arcade**

**Archère:** a loop-hole

**Bailey:** or **ward**, the courtyard of a castle which is defended

**Ballista:** an engine worked by tension and used for throwing projectiles

**Barbican:** a small advanced fortification used to protect a gateway. These outer fortifications acted as a protection for the main gate, and were often sited on the opposite side of the ditch, astride the approach to

*A plan of Goodrich Castle illustrates the use made of a natural defensible site, and the elaboration of gatehouses and barbicans characteristic of its period*

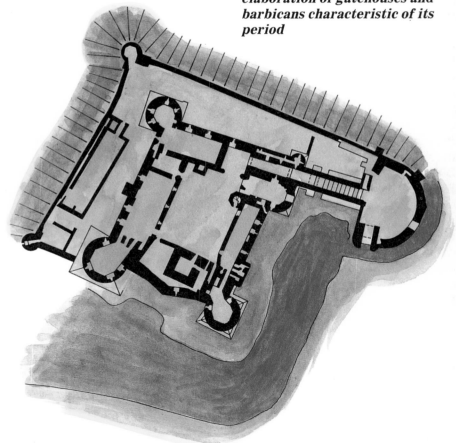

the drawbridge. Sizes varied greatly, but their purpose was to delay any attack on the main gate, thereby giving the defenders time to assemble and organise. Some barbicans were joined to the main gatehouse by tall curtain walls on both sides, with both parapets and parados to provide archers not only with the opportunity of firing down onto any attackers who had breached the barbican, but also outwards towards the field.

**Barmkin:** another word for **bailey**, used in connection with pele towers

**Bartizan:** or **eschaugette**, a turret that projects from the top of a wall or tower

**Bastide:** military settlement laid out along Roman lines in southern France in the 14th century

**Batter:** an inward slope to a wall face

**Belfry:** or **beffroi**, a seige tower

**Berm:** ledge sited at the base of a' wall to stop *débris* falling into a moat or wet ditch

**Brattice:** or **bretèche**, a movable wooden structure or tower, usually used to defend the end of a bridge

**Burgh:** Anglo-Saxon fortified township

**Casemate:** gallery built outside the base of a wall, fitted with loop-holes through which the archers could fire; also used for a vaulted chamber in the base of a tower from which flanking fire could be directed

**Castellan:** or **constable**, the commander of a castle, the official in charge in the absence of its owner

**Cat:** popular name for a **penthouse**, a movable shelter for miners and rams; also known as a **sow** or **mouse**

**Chamber:** a private room

**Chemise:** a wall built closely around a **donjon**

**Constable:** *see* **castellan**

**Corbel:** a projecting stone that acts as a support for a beam; several tiers of corbels may be used to carry a parapet or tower

**Counter castle:** a castle erected by the beseigers to protect their operations

**Coursière:** wooden roofing over a wall-walk

**Crenel:** or **crenelle**, one of the gaps or square notches between the raised parts in the castellation of a battlement

**Curtain:** or **courtine**, the proper name for a length of wall linking two towers. From earliest times, basic protection was provided by walls that enclosed the dwellings, initially built from timber, later from stone. The timber walls were backed by ramparts of earth for additional solidity and protection against battering rams. Later this earthen support would have been completely encased in timber for added support, thus enabling the frontal timbers to project above the earth backing, which itself formed a convenient sentry-walk, to form a breastwork.

The stone walls which succeeded the timber had enough mass to be able to withstand battering rams on their own; they also had the added advantages of being fireproof and able to accommodate a sentry-walk within their own thickness. The outer facing wall continued beyond the main body of the wall would then form a parapet and if the inner facing wall was similarly extended, this inner parapet was called a parados.

Thus the essential castle element, the curtain wall, was developed. Further additions or embellishments followed; some sentry-walks were covered with lead so as to protect the masonry from the penetrating rain, and drain holes were also built in, as were holes to carry the beams of a hoard. Parapets became battlemented with crenels (the **u** in the parapet) and merlons, which continue the parapet in between the crenels. Swing shutters were later added to the crenels for extra security, and from the beginning of the 13th century loop holes were added for the archers in the middle of the merlons, which were themselves also surmounted by an overhanging lip to deflect arrows ricocheting.

**Donjon:** medieval word of French origins for a keep.

**Drawbridge:** there are four main types, from the simplest gangplank across the ditch or moat and which could be very easily retracted, to the only slightly more complex lifting bridges which were hinged on the castle side and raised by chains pulled in from a room above the gatehouse. This simple arrangement provided additional protection, as when raised the bridge formed an additional wooden door.

For larger gate passages requiring longer and heavier drawbridges to span wider ditches, which could not be manually hauled up by pulling on chains, a swing or turning bridge was used. It employed the same principle as the lifting

*The entrance and double drawbridge of Chaumont Castle. Chaumont was built from 1465 onwards, on the ruins of a former fortress founded in the 10th century by Eudes I, Count of Blois. The Château is situated on a hillside dominating the left bank of the Loire*

bridge, but was extended backwards into the gatehouse and pivoted at its threshold. A counterweight enabled the back of the bridge to swing down into a pit and the front to rise up, again forming an extra door. The pit into which the back of the bridge swung also provided an extra obstacle for the attackers. When down, the bridge was held in position at the back end by a bar, which slid under the counterbalance. When the bridge was raised, a second bar slid across its outer face from an adjacent tower to hold it in position.

By the 14th century, the drawbridge had developed still further, with long beams, counterbalanced on their inner (castle) ends, and pivoted just above the gate opening at its threshold. Projecting horizontally from the gatehouse, they had chains affixed to their outer ends which ran down to the outer end corners of the drawbridge. These beams, when swung down by the counterbalances, raised the drawbridge with them. In order to hold the bridge tight against the gate opening, the beams fell back into the slots cut into the stonework of the gatehouse. Such bridges were called bascula bridges.

**Embrasure:** a space hollowed into a thick wall, which allows the archer to stand closer to a loop

**Enceinte:** the complete circuit of walls and towers around a fortified place

**Escalade:** the assault of a castle made by climbing its walls

**Eschaugette:** *see* **bartizan**

**Fausse braye:** a line of defence along the floor of a ditch at the base of the walls

**Forebuilding:** a building projecting from the face of a keep, containing the entrance stair

**Garderobe:** latrine

**Gatehouse:** every castle had its gatehouse, symbolising its character, its defences and its power. Although originally there would have been timber gatehouses, even from excavations it is not possible to judge accurately their size or construction; but assuming that they were of a similar nature to the early stone constructions, they would have been square or nearly so.

Some early stone gatehouses had pilaster buttresses; size obviously varied greatly but could be up to 15m (50ft) square and two or three storeys high. The entrance passage to the gatehouse was defended by a drawbridge, wooden doors and in most instances by at least one portcullis. The passage then passed under the gate-

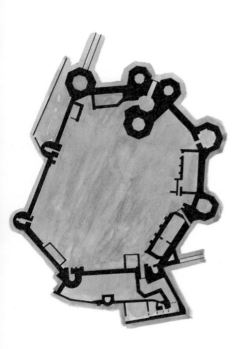

*A plan of the gatehouse at Denbigh Castle, North Wales, seen in context with the rest of the Castle, which it dominates. It is a most remarkable gatehouse, being triple-towered. It was built for Henry de Lacy, Earl of Lincoln, a close associate of Edward I*

house, where it was generally further protected by a vault, against fire.

At the end of the 12th century, gatehouses began to appear with small towers, square or round, placed on both sides of the gate. A little later on these towers were joined above the entrance passage, thereby forming a gatehouse which had two protecting towers which overlooked the approach to the castle. These tower gatehouses provided quite good accommodation and were most usually inhabited by the constable of the castle. By the early 13th century, they were often further protected by barbicans and drawbridges.

**Glacis:** *see* **talus**

**Hall:** a formal reception room used for the holding of courts and the entertaining of guests

**Hoard:** or **hourd**, an overhanging wooden gallery projecting from the parapet which enables the defenders to drop things on those below

**Jamb:** the side of a door or

window; also in Scotland, the projecting wing of a tower house

**Keep:** the main tower of a castle, the strongest part and last resort, often isolated and capable of independent defence

**Lintel:** top piece of a door or window opening

**List:** interval between two lines of concentric walls

**Loop:** a narrow opening in a wall through which the defenders can discharge their arrows, and later, gunshot

**Machicolation:** a stone version of a hoard

**Mangonel:** an engine worked by torsion and used for throwing projectiles

**Manlet:** mobile screen which gives protective cover to the besiegers

**Merlon:** the short solid part of a parapet between two crenelles

**Meurtrière:** hole over a passageway for dropping things on those below

**Motte:** a steep, large, artificial or natural mound of earth for the support of a timber tower

**Mouse:** *see* **cat**

**Oratory:** a small private chamber for prayer

**Palisade:** a fence of wooden stakes

**Parados:** a stone breastwork comprising crenelles and merlons on top that protects the rear of a sentry-walk; generally referred to as battlements

**Parapet:** like a **parados** but protecting the front of a sentry-walk

**Penthouse:** *see* **cat**

**Pilaster:** a flat, decorative buttress, often found on keeps

**Piscina:** a stone basin in a chapel, used for rinsing sacred vessels

**Portcullis:** wooden grille that slides vertically in grooves cut into the stonework of a gate passage. This was, in effect, a gate which worked on the principle of sliding down into position from above, guided by grooves cut into the stonework at each side. The portcullis comprised a frame of strong timbers, which were held together by iron nails. As the portcullis would be needed to drop quickly in an emergency, the lower ends of the vertical timbers were shaped to a point and also covered with iron. Although the portcullis timbers formed an open grid, this was stronger than a door, in that it was not hinged and thus it could not be burst open.

The portcullis was raised by a windlass housed in a room

*The portcullis raising gear housed in a room above the gate passage at Cahir Castle, and* inset *the entrance and portcullis of Warwick Castle*

immediately above the gate passage, into which the upper part of the portcullis protruded when it was opened up.

**Postern:** small exit gate also called a **sallyport**

**Putlog holes:** holes left by the withdrawal of timbers used to secure the scaffolding

**Ravelin:** a triangular-shaped outwork, sited in a ditch in front of a curtain wall

**Sedilia:** a row of stone seats set against the south wall of a chapel

**Slighting:** deliberate damage to a castle to prevent further use

**Solar:** private room used by the lord or his family

**Sow:** *see* **cat**

**Talus:** sloping wall, which is thicker at its base

**Trèbuchet:** a siege engine worked by counterpoise

**Vault:** an arched stone roof; a **barrel vault** has a semi-circular arch, and a **Gothic vault** has a pointed arch

**Vice:** a spiral staircase built into the thickness of the wall

**Wall tower:** the all-important curtain wall defences linked the wall towers together and although it is not certain when these towers first made their appearance, there is evidence to suggest that a few wooden structures date from earthwork castles; 12th-century examples of wall towers sug-

gest a purely military purpose, having open backs and no accommodation facilities. This changed in the 13th century, when King John rebuilt the wall towers of Dover Castle. These solid stone-based **D**-section towers were closed at the back and had an upper hollow portion which could be used for storage or accommodation. The back of the **D** faced inwards to the bailey and the rounded side faced outwards. Later towers embodied multi-storey accommodation, most usually with short flights of stairs built in the thickness of the walls. These wall towers formed an integral part of the basic structure of the castles throughout the Middle Ages. Curtain walls and wall towers were often separate entities, with no access to the tower from the sentry-walk other than at ground level. In other instances, the sentry-walk was continued round the outside of the tower, again affording no entrance to the tower itself, while occasionally the sentry-walk passed through the tower.

**Window seat:** a stone seat built into the jamb of a window

**Ward:** *see* **bailey**

**Yett:** an iron gate found in tower houses

*An aerial view of Dover, with its
impressive wall towers*

Superlaunch Ltd thank the many owners and custodians of castles featured for their generous assistance with the production of this book, and Andrew Wright for additional artworks

*Below:* **Berkeley Castle, fortress home of the Berkeley family for nearly 850 years**